The Difference Between Horses, Donkeys and Mules

Children's Science & Nature

BABY PROFESSOR

EDUCATION KIDS

Speedy Publishing LLC
40 E. Main St. #1156
Newark, DE 19711
www.speedypublishing.com
Copyright 2016

Kids, in this book you will learn interesting facts about horses, donkeys and mules. They may look the same and come from the same family but they have important differences. Read on and discover their differences.

Let's check out
for these amazing
farm animals.

HORSES Have you experienced riding on a horse?

Scientific Name: Equus ferus caballus

During 50 million years, horses evolved from smaller creatures. Horses have four legs. They have had a long, close relationship with humans. Horses can be used as a form of transportation. Over the years, they have served people.

Horses come in different breeds. They are of different colors, sizes, and skills. Horses perform different work depending on their breed. Horses have different names based on their ages. For example, a colt is the name given to a male horse which is less than four years old while a foal is the name given to a horse less than one year old. Ponies are small horses.

Horses can sleep while standing. They eat hay and grasses, for they are herbivores. They are known as grazing animals. They also enjoy eating legumes and grains.

Horses are able to see about 360 degrees at one time because their big eyes are located on the sides of their head. A male horse is known as stallion while a female horse is called a mare.

DONKEYS

Scientific Name:
Equus africanus asinus

Are you familiar with their "hee-haw" neighs? Have you heard their clunky hooves?

Around 5,000 years ago, donkeys were bred and tamed in Egypt and Mesopotamia. A donkey's wild ancestor is the African wild ass. They belong to a different species from horses, and they are smaller. Donkeys are sometimes called "burros" and "asses".

Donkeys are slower than horses, but they are strong and industrious. They are dependable. In fact, in poor countries, donkeys are used to plow the fields and do other hard work. They are believed to be related to zebras.

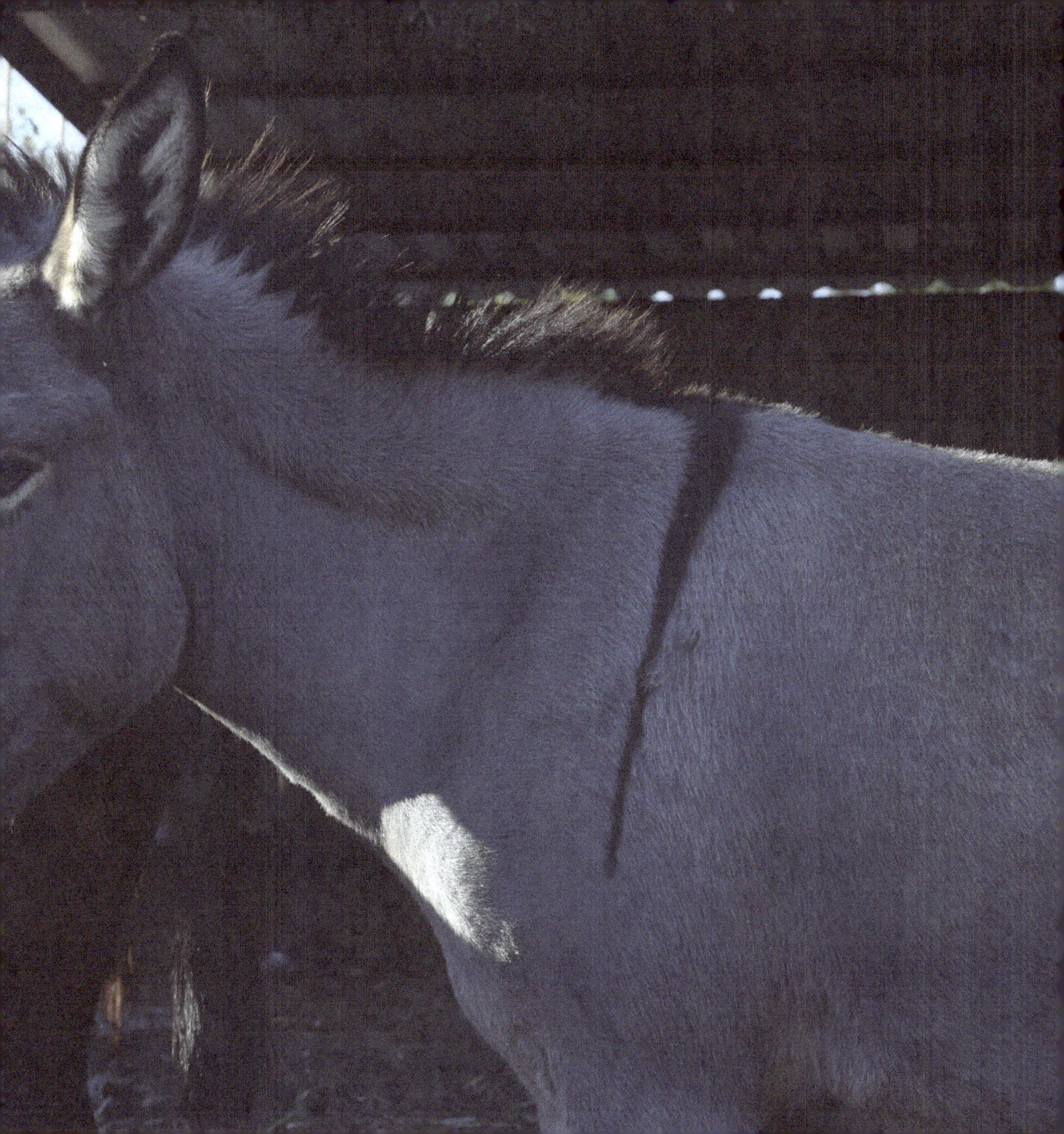

More donkeys are found in China than in other countries around the world. They are considered as pets in the United States. Some Americans take mate donkeys with horses to breed mules. Mules are bigger than a donkey. A male donkey is known as "jack" while the female is called "jenny".

Donkeys have stiffer manes compared to horses. Their ears are longer than horses ears, but horses have longer faces.

MULES

Scientific NAME:
Equus Mule

They are a cross-bred
between a female horse
and a male donkey.
Yes, mules are a hybrid.
They are called jack
or jackass. The young
of a male horse and
a female donkey, on
the other hand, is
called a "hinny". A
female donkey is
called a "jenny".

Mules are brave. They have served armies in many wars, even in the recent wars in Afghanistan and Iraq.

The hooves of a mule are tougher and are more protected from diseases. Since a mule is a mix of a female horse and a male donkey, it has amazing characteristics. It has the intelligence of a donkey and the power of a horse.

What's the main difference between a horse, donkey and a mule? Amazingly, it's the genetics. Horses have 64 chromosomes while donkeys have 62 chromosomes. When they are cross-bred, the mule and the hinny are left with 63 chromosomes. This is interesting! Who would have imagined it?

A mule cannot have
children because
it has an irregular
chromosome count.
Mules can't reproduce
naturally. Mules are
also hard working
animals, like the
horses and donkeys.

Did you enjoy
reading? Share this
to your friends.

المسار الرئيسي
إلى منطقة قصر البنت
Main Trail to Qasr
al-Bint Area (The Basin)
مسار المذبح
High Place of Sacrifice Trail

Visit
BABY PROFESSOR
EDUCATION KIDS
www.BabyProfessorBooks.com
to download Free Baby Professor eBooks
and view our catalog of new and exciting
Children's Books